MEMORIES OF HOME

FROM Dad and Mother
6/15/79 Robinson

CHARLEVOIX "The Beautiful" **MICHIGAN**

To Allyn and Jo
on your Anniversary

POSTMASTER: MERCHANDISE. THIS PARCEL MAY BE OPENED FOR POSTAL INSPECTION IF NECESSARY.

MEMORIES
OF

HOME

Compiled by
CAESAR JOHNSON

Illustrated by
MARVIN BESUNDER

Published by
The C. R. Gibson Company
Norwalk, Connecticut

We have gathered from many writings those selections which recall familiar memories. It is the little memories, the various bits and pieces, which make up all our lives. There are the fond memories of childhood which remain with us forever. There are the happy memories of special days and special people and special places. Home is a very special memory to each of us, and we hope that these selections will bring back your memories of home.

A complete list of acknowledgments will be found at the end of this book.

Copyright © MCMLXX by
The C. R. Gibson Company, Norwalk, Connecticut
All rights reserved
Printed in the United States of America
Library of Congress Catalog Card Number: 78-91818
SBN: 8378-1782-X

CONTENTS

I
LAUGHTER OF CHILDREN 7

II
THINGS THAT ARE FAMILIAR 21

III
MEMORIES THROUGH THE YEAR 35

IV
SWEET DREAMS 49

V
ECHOES THAT REMAIN 59

VI
THE HEARTH OF HOME 69

LAUGHTER OF CHILDREN

Laughter of children brings
The kitchen down with laughter.
While the old kettle sings
Laughter of children brings
To a boil all savory things.
Higher than beam or rafter,
Laughter of children brings
The kitchen down with laughter.

BARBARA HOWES

The gentleman who lives next door
Comes in to visit me,
And weighty questions we discuss
The while we drink our tea.

"What makes fleas always bother dogs?"
"Don't cats have funny eyes?"
"Do all the other birdies know
That owls are very wise?"
"Do grubworms curl themselves up tight
So they can warm their feet?"
"What makes the onions smell so queer
And roses smell so sweet?"
"Which do you think you'd rather be,
A toad-frog or a sheep?"
"Do little fishes close their eyes
And snuggle down to sleep?"

The gentleman who lives next door,
Although he is only three,
Discloses my vast ignorance
Each time he visits me.

      SEIGNIORA LAUNE

  Give me no mansions ivory white
  Nor palaces of pearl and gold;
  Give me a child for all delight,
    Just four years old.

  Give me no wings of rosy shine
  Nor snowy raiment, fold on fold,
  Give me a little boy all mine,
    Just four years old.

      KATHERINE TYNAN

  Sweet childish days, that were as long
  As twenty days are now.

    ALFRED, LORD TENNYSON

A child should have pockets —
Supposing on the road
He runs across a beetle,
Or a lizard, or a toad?
However will he carry them?
Whatever will he do
If he hasn't got a pocket
To put them into?

A child should have a pocket
On which he fairly dotes!
Not one or two, but many
In his little waistcoats —
And one will be for money
He finds on the road,
And one for cakes and cookies
And one for hoptoads!

    SUSAN ADGER WILLIAMS

Dear Santa Claus, do you suppose
That you could send to me,
Two trains with tracks this Christmas Eve
If I'm as good as can be?

You see, Dear Mr. Santa Claus,
My daddy likes to play
With all my things, but most of all
He likes the track to lay!

Dear Santa Claus, if you can send me
Two trains, why don't you see,
My dad can play with his own train,
And leave my train for me!

    AGNES CARR

Oh, for boyhood's time of June,
Crowding years in one brief moon.
  JOHN GREENLEAF WHITTIER

LAUGHTER OF CHILDREN

Nine-o'clock Bell!
Nine-o'clock Bell!
All the small children and big ones as well,
Pulling their stockings up, snatching their hats,
Cheeking and grumbling and giving back-chats,
Laughing and quarreling, dropping their things,
These at a snail's pace and those upon wings,
Lagging behind a bit, running ahead,
Waiting at corners for lights to turn red,
Some of them scurrying,
Others not worrying,
Carelessly trudging or anxiously hurrying,
All through the streets they are coming pell-mell
At the Nine-o'clock
  Nine-o'clock
  Nine-o'clock
      Bell!

ELEANOR FARJEON

I had a feeling in my neck,
And on the sides were two big bumps;
I couldn't swallow anything
At all because I had the mumps.

And Mother tied it with a piece,
And then she tied up Will and John,
And no one else but Dick was left
That didn't have a mump rag on.

He teased us and laughed at us,
And said, whenever he went by,
"It's vinegar and lemon-drops
And pickles!" just to make us cry.

But Tuesday Dick was very sad
And cried because his neck was sore,
And not a one said sour things
To anybody any more.

ELIZABETH MADOX ROBERTS

When the voices of children are heard on the green
And laughing is heard on the hill,
My heart is at rest within my breast
    And everything else is still.

'Then come home, my children, the sun is gone down
And the dews of night arise;
Come, come, leave off play, and let us away
Till the morning appears in the skies.'

'No, no, let us play, for it is yet day
And we cannot go to sleep;
Besides in the sky the little birds fly
And the hills are all cover'd with sheep.'

'Well, well, go and play till the light fades away
And then go home to bed.'
The little ones leaped and shouted and laughed
    And all the hills echoed.

                              WILLIAM BLAKE

      Easy, wind!
      Go softly here!
      She is small
      And very dear.

      She is young
      And cannot say
      Words to chase
      The wind away.

      She is new
      To walking so
      Wind, be kind
      And gently blow.

      On her ruffled head
      On grass and clover
      Easy, wind . . .
      She'll tumble over!

          FRANCES M. FROST

LAUGHTER OF CHILDREN

Dig We Must

My wife, Marguerite, was born in Caen, France; I was born in Fargo, North Dakota. Though separated by 5,000 miles of prairie, ocean, moderately low mountains, rivers, and disparate cultures, our childhoods were similar in one respect: we both dug holes in the family gardens. The holes themselves were largely incidental; it was what we found at the other end that counted. What I mean is that we diggers never lost the opportunity to announce to anybody who would care to listen that if we dug down far enough we'd soon come out on the other side of the world, in the exotic land of China.

No hole ever dug exceeded eighteen inches in depth, but it is safe to say that until the age of twelve or thereabouts, our absolute confidence in the outlandish wonders we would encounter if, by magic or muscle, we ever succeeded in piercing the remaining 7,927 miles of granite, balsite, and molten core, never diminished a single iota.

Some thirty-five years later we inhabit the somewhat less exotic precincts of Forest Hills, New York. The other day we noticed one of the neighboring kids spading out some kind of hole in his back yard, and as he puffed, sweated, and belabored the dirt, he declaimed to several nearby pals the ancient childhood fiction of the hole direct to China.

Fiction? I could hardly wait to get home and haul down the atlas. What part of China, I wanted to know, would this under-aged excavator of New York bang into as soon as he dug through the mucko and the Moho, and emerged on the other side? I got my answer in about three minutes flat. He'd end up in the South Indian Ocean, about 700 miles off the southwest coast of Australia, missing the nearest Chinese land by about 4,200 miles. I dug down from Caen and found myself in the South Pacific, about 400 miles southeast of New Zealand. A perpendicular hole from Fargo, North Dakota, dumped me again in the South Indian Ocean, about 1,500 miles from the nearest substantial land — Australia or Antarctica, take your choice.

The fever mounted. I did a number of further calculations. I dug down from Montreal, Rome, Jerusalem, Addis Ababa, Accra, and the Cape of Good Hope, and came up for air in such unlikely spots as the Tasman Sea, the south coast of Papua, and the Pacific Ocean somewhere north of Hawaii.

At last I halted. If there was a snip of dry land anywhere on this whirling mudball where a kid could dig his hole and reach China, I was going to find it — by the numbers.

The answer came some six sheets later — sheets of messy, but undeniably high-class calculations.

Kids of the world, I can here and now report that from parts of only five countries on this globe can you dig straight down to China: Argentina, Chile, Paraguay, a minuscule unpopulated bump of southern Bolivia, and the Falkland Islands. And here, for your next spading expedition, I present a few of my select digging spots in the Southern Hemisphere:

Los Angeles, Chile: Dig here and end up on the Great Wall of China, a hop and a skip from the town of Tingpien, Kansu Province.

Falkland Islands: Dig here and end up in Northern Manchuria, smack dab in the Great Khingan Mountains, a couple of hundred miles from absolutely nowhere.

Villa Federal, Argentina: Dig down here and end up, feet first, in little old Shanghai.

Mount Lipez, Bolivia (17,398 feet): Dig down here and come right out into the cellars of Macao, the Portuguese gambling colony on the South China coast where, with a little bit of luck, you can cover digging expenses, and maybe even have a yuan or two left over for a chow mein dinner.

Confuso River, Paraguay: Dig along the banks of this waterway northwest of Asunción, end up in Taipei, Formosa, right in Chiang Kai-shek's lap.

LAUGHTER OF CHILDREN

We live in an age of deviousness, an age of overskills, and I know that any American kid with an ounce of inventiveness ought to be able to dig his hole slantwise (like those oil-well bimbos in Texas) and get to China from any old spot on this crust. It wouldn't count, though. In the China-digging game no cheating is permitted. You gotta be a straight digger. Any kid can tell you that.

LAWRENCE LEVINE

You have to ask children and birds how cherries and strawberries taste.

JOHANN WOLFGANG VON GOETHE

The Little Whistler

My mother whistled softly,
My father whistled bravely,
My brother whistled merrily,
And I tried all day long!
I blew my breath inwards,
I blew my breath outwards,
But all you heard was breath blowing
And not a bit of song!

But today I heard a bluebird,
A happy, young, and new bird,
Whistling in the apple tree —
He'd just discovered how!
Then quick I blew my breath in,
And gay I blew my breath out,
And sudden I blew three wild notes —
And I can whistle now!

FRANCES FROST

Ah! happy years! Once more who would not be a boy!

GEORGE GORDON, LORD BYRON

I remember the gleams and glooms that dart
Across the school-boy brain;
The song and the silence in the heart,
That in part are prophecies, and in part
Are longings wild and vain.
And the voice of that fitful song
Sings on, and is never still:
"A boy's will is the wind's will,
And the thoughts of youth are long, long thoughts."
HENRY WADSWORTH LONGFELLOW

I know he's coming by this sign,—
The baby's almost wild!
See how he laughs and crows and starts —
Heaven bless the merry child!
He's father's self in face and limb,
And father's heart is strong in him.
Shout, baby, shout! and clap thy hands,
For father on the threshold stands.
HARRIET OAKLEY

The Secret Cavern

Underneath the boardwalk, way, way back,
There's a splendid cavern, big and black —
If you want to get there, you must crawl
Underneath the posts and steps and all
When I've finished paddling, there I go —
None of all the other children know!

There I keep my treasures in a box —
Shells and colored glass and queer-shaped rocks,
In a secret hiding place I've made,
Hollowed out with clamshells and a spade,
Marked with yellow pebbles in a row —
None of all the other children know!
MARGARET WIDDEMER

LAUGHTER OF CHILDREN

There must have been some time in my life when I played baseball with nine men on a team, but surely it was not on our block. We played with as many kids as were around, and I don't think there were eighteen kids on the block. We always carefully looked at the bat to make sure the label was up, because if the label wasn't up, it would split the bat. Is there any truth in this? I don't know. It was an article of faith, and any kid who didn't turn the label up was screamed at until he did.

ROBERT PAUL SMITH

The Circus-Day Parade

Oh, the circus-day parade! How the bugles played
    and played!
And how the glossy horses tossed their flossy manes,
    and neighed,
As the rattle and the rhyme of the tenor-drummer's
    time
Filled all the hungry hearts of us with melody sublime!

How the grand band-wagon shone with a splendor
    all its own,
And glittered with a glory that our dreams had
    never known!
And how the boys behind, high and low of every kind,
Marched in unconscious capture, with a rapture
    undefined!

How the horsemen, two and two, with their plumes
    of white and blue,
And crimson, gold and purple, nodding by at me
    and you,
Waved the banners that they bore, as the Knights in
    days of yore,
Till our glad eyes gleamed and glistened like the
    spangles that they wore!

JAMES WHITCOMB RILEY

"I saw an elephant walking down the road.
He had a book and was going to school.
He carried a satchel to hold his lunch —
APRIL FOOL!

"I saw your grandmother and your aunt
Fishing for suckers in the mill-stream pool.
They'd caught a dozen and maybe more —
APRIL FOOL!

"Mercy! whoever has mended your shirt?
The needle's still there and the thread and the spool.
Didn't you feel them there at the hem?
APRIL FOOL!

      ELIZABETH COATSWORTH

Animals crackers, and cocoa to drink,
That is the finest suppers, I think;
When I'm grown up and can have what I please
I think I shall always insist upon these.

What do you choose when you're offered a treat?
When Mother says, "What would you like best to eat?"
Is it waffles and syrup, or cinnamon toast?
It's cocoa and animals that I love the most!

The kitchen's the cosiest place that I know:
The kettle is singing, the stove is aglow,
And there in the twilight, how jolly to see
The cocoa and animals waiting for me.

      CHRISTOPHER MORLEY

Mud

Mud is very nice to feel
All squishy-squash between the toes!
I'd rather wade in wiggly mud
Than smell a yellow rose.

    POLLY CHASE BOYDEN

LAUGHTER OF CHILDREN

Everyone grumbled. The sky was grey.
We had nothing to do and nothing to say.
We were nearing the end of a dismal day,
And there seemed to be nothing beyond,
> THEN
  Daddy fell into the pond!

And everyone's face grew merry and bright,
And Timothy danced for sheer delight.
"Give me the camera, quick, oh quick!
He's crawling out of the duckweed." Click!

Then the gardener suddenly slapped his knee,
And doubled up, shaking silently,
And the ducks all quacked as if they were daft
And it sounded as if the old drake laughed.

O, there wasn't a thing that didn't respond.
> WHEN
  Daddy fell into the pond!

ALFRED NOYES

When I was a boy of fourteen, my father
was so ignorant I could hardly stand to
have the old man around. But when I got
to be twenty-one, I was astonished at how
much he had learned in seven years.

MARK TWAIN

His words were magic and his heart was true,
And everywhere he wandered he was blessed
Out of all ancient men my childhood knew
I choose him and I mark him for the best.
Of all authoritative liars, too,
I crown him loveliest.

EDWIN ARLINGTON ROBINSON

How do you like to go up in a swing,
    Up in the air so blue?
Oh, I do think it the pleasantest thing
    Ever a child can do!

Up in the air and over the wall,
    Till I can see so wide,
Rivers and trees and cattle and all
    Over the countryside —

Till I look down on the garden green,
    Down on the roof so brown —
Up in the air I go flying again,
    Up in the air and down!

            ROBERT LOUIS STEVENSON

When my birthday was coming
Little Brother had a secret.
He kept it for days and days
And just hummed a little tune
    when I asked him.
But one night it rained,
And I woke and heard him crying;
Then he told me.
"I planted two lumps of sugar
    in your garden
Because you love it so frightfully.
I thought there would be a whole sugar
    tree for your birthday.
And now it will be all melted."
Oh, the darling!

            KATHERINE MANSFIELD

LAUGHTER OF CHILDREN

THINGS THAT ARE FAMILIAR

Simple Things

Give me simple things close to my home,
The things that are familiar, old and dear,
I do not have to wander far, or roam
The Seven Seas — when I have splendor here.

Give me a crackling flame upon the grate
And the warm smell of bread upon the fire.
I do not have to ride abroad in state
To find the very core of heart's desire.

A shining tea pot — friendly hands to pour
And jam that smells of grapes from our own vine.
Could any noble king desire more?
I am a king myself, for these are mine.

Let those who will seek promised lands afar,
For treasures so remote I shed no tear.
Why should I strive to reach a distant star
When heaven with all its beauty is right here?

DOROTHY DAY

When mother comes each morning
    She wears her oldest things,
She doesn't make a rustle,
    She hasn't any rings;
She says, "Good-morning, chickies,
    It's such a lovely day,
Let's go into the garden
    And have a game of play!"

When mother comes at bed-time
    Her evening dress she wears,
She tells us each a story
    When we have said our prayers;
And if there is a party
    She looks so shiny bright
It's like a lovely fairy
    Dropped in to say good-night.

ROSE FYLEMAN

The baby takes to her bed at night
A one-eyed rabbit that once was white,
A watch that came from a cracker, I think;
And a lidless inkpot that never held ink.
And the secret is locked in the tiny breast
Of why she loves these and leaves the rest.

And I give a loving glance as I go
To three brass pots on the shelf in a row;
To my grandfather's grandfather's loving cup
And a bandy-legged chair I once picked up.
And I can't, for the life of me, make you see
Why just these things are a part of me!

J. H. MACNAIR

Memory is the treasury and guardian of all things.
CICERO

How dear to my heart are the scenes of my childhood
  When fond recollections presents them to view!
The orchard, the meadow, the deep-tangled wildwood,
  And every loved spot which my infancy knew.

                           SAMUEL WOODWORTH

Prelude

The winter evening settles down
With smells of steaks in passageways.
Six o'clock.
The burnt-out end of smoky days.
And now a gusty shower wraps
The grimy scraps
Of withered leaves about your feet
And newspapers from vacant lots;
The showers beat
On broken blinds and chimney-pots,
And at the corner of the street
A lonely cab-horse steams and stamps.
And then the lighting of the lamps.

                           T. S. ELIOT

Let's have a picnic out-of-doors!
Let's make the beds, and do the chores,
Let's pack the basket high and take
The peach pie and the johnnycake,
And lemons, sugar, spoons, a cup:
Don't hesitate to fill it up.

Let's have a picnic out-of-doors!
We may not steam to foreign shores;
But to the meadow we can take
Our peach pie and our johnnycake,
And see the birds and trees — and eat,
And find existence there quite sweet.

                    MARY CAROLYN DAVIES

THINGS THAT ARE FAMILIAR

The attic window's in the ceiling;
   You only see the clouds go by;
And when I'm there I have a feeling
   Of being very near the sky.

The attic air is warm and dusty,
   And there are boxes full of things,
And rods of iron, rather rusty,
   And beds and trunks and curtain rings.

I often like to go and play there;
   I take my story-book and toys;
It seems so very far away there,
   From all the people and the noise.

But when the blue behind the skylight
   Has faded to a dingy grey,
And a mouse scrabbles in the twilight,
   I leave my things and go away.

                        ROSE FYLEMAN

I love my queer cellar with its dusty smell,
Its misty smell like smoke-fringes
From clouds blowing past;
With its shelves of jams and goodies,
With its boxes . . . barrels . . .
Woodpiles here and there.
There is a passageway
To an unknown room
Where bins holds carrots and things.
There are glass doors that bang
And cobweb windows.
I love the quietness of my cellar
Thinking in the dark.
My cellar has apples in its breath,
Potatoes even,
That smell of earth.

                        HILDA CONKLING

Country Lanes

There's nothing like our country lanes with all
   their shady trees,
The leaves and branches stirring high above us in
   the breeze,
The sweet, rich smell of growing things enhance
   the beauty there,
As flowers bright and beautiful leave fragrance
   in the air.
The branches of the stalwart trees sway gently
   overhead,
The green grass makes a carpet soft along the roads
   we tread;
A soothing breeze stirs daily here refreshing
   passersby
Who linger longingly beneath the leaf-flecked,
   country sky.
The birds sing merrily on high within their
   cosy nests,
The bees and insects softly hum while on their
   daily quests,
Where many a city family go to ease their aches
   and pains
By picnicking on Sundays in our shady country
   lanes.

                        LAURA MUNRO

My dog's so furry I've not seen
His face for years and years:
His eyes are buried out of sight,
I only guess his ears.

When people ask me for his breed,
I do not know or care:
He has the beauty of them all
Hidden beneath his hair.

                HERBERT ASQUITH

THINGS THAT ARE FAMILIAR

I love it; and who shall dare
To chide me for loving that old armchair.

ELIZA COOK

I remember, I remember
The house where I was born,
The little window where the sun
Came peeping in at morn;
He never came a wink too soon
Nor brought a day too long.

THOMAS HOOD

When I was a child seven years old, my friends on a holiday filled my pocket with coppers. I went directly to a shop where they sold toys for children, and being charmed with the sound of a whistle that I met by the way in the hands of another boy, I voluntarily offered and gave all my money for one. I then came home, and went whistling all over the house, much pleased with my whistle, but disturbing all the family.

BENJAMIN FRANKLIN

Do You Save String?

I have just taken a complete inventory of our house from top to bottom, which is the only way I can get into it these days, and I have made a list of the things that people keep. They may be grouped roughly as follows:

1. *Things that go on things,* like the tops of jelly glasses, covers of peanut-butter jars, caps of bottles, lids of pots, and saucers to put upside down over other saucers with things in them.

2. *Things that come off things,* such as buttons, buckles, suitcase straps, hinges, a bolt from Junior's bicycle, the

nozzle of the garden hose, some screws that fell out of the vacuum cleaner, dear, and this nut I found lying under the car when I tried to start it this morning.

3. *Things that other things came in,* such as paper bags, egg cartons, wicker baskets, round tin boxes that contained preserved fruits — no real thing-keeper can ever resist a round tin box — and any kind of empty jar at all.

4. *Things that seem a shame to throw away,* such as a deck of playing cards with only three or four missing, the top of a pair of silk pajamas that could be used for cleaning rags or something, this vest that is still as good as ever even if the suit is all gone, and a left-hand fur mitten if we could ever find the right-hand one.

5. *Things in the cellar,* such as between thirty and forty flowerpots which I knock over every time I go downstairs, the handle of an ice-cream freezer, a stack of tomato flats from last spring with the dirt still in them, and several empty barrels in case we ever have to move again.

6. *Things to keep things from going in and out,* such as old vacuum-bottle corks to plug up mouse holes, some short pieces of felt weather stripping, and a triangular section of wire mesh left over from the new porch screens which might come in handy to patch them sometime if they ever wear out.

7. *Things that have a certain sentimental value,* like the snapshots of that summer in the Adirondacks, wedding announcements, high-school diplomas, that derby hat you wore in college, and all last year's Christmas cards.

8. *Things that are too nice to use,* such as the crocheted bedspread that Great-Aunt Effie made with her own two hands, that set of hand-painted demitasse cups that were a wedding present from the Alvords, and a bottle of Napoleon brandy we've been saving for ten years for some special occasion.

COREY FORD

THINGS THAT ARE FAMILIAR

A Child upon the Stair

Now when I stand upon the stair alone
And listen, I can hear a quiet stir
Like even breathing, or a whispered drone,
A sound that any little noise would blur.
I know that there is something in this hall,
That climbs the waiting stairs and then goes down
On silent feet, or clings hard to the wall,
As though it loved the old and faded brown.
Sometimes I feel that I, myself, can fly
If I stand very still upon the stair,
Believing that there is no reason why
I cannot trust my body to the air . . .
Do other children find their stairs so near
To things that grown-ups say cannot be here?

CAROLYN HALL

My Mother's Clothes

When I was small, my mother's clothes
All seemed so kind to me!
I hid my face amid the folds
As safe as safe could be.

The gown that she had on
To me seemed shining bright,
For woven in that simple stuff
Were comfort and delight.

Yes, everything she wore
Received my hopes and fears,
And even the garments of her soul
Contained my smiles and tears.

Then softly will I touch
This dress she used to wear.
The old-time comfort lingers yet,
My smiles and tears are there.

A tenderness abides
Though laid so long away,
And I must kiss their empty folds,
So comfortable are they.
                    ANNA HEMPSTEAD BRANCH

In an Old Parlor

Life-sized portraits on the wall
Painted, so long ago;
Sea shells on a table
Brought home by wandering Joe.

A small stand in a corner
Holds the Bible, heavily bound,
Records of marriages, births and deaths
Between its leaves are found.

A few old books and albums,
Waxed flowers, and hair wreathes,
A hair cloth sofa, and old arm-chair
With a foot-rest beneath.

A scene stamped on my memory;
And I'll not soon forget
The old room with its secrets
Where shadows linger yet.
                    AGNES FLEMING

What makes a garden?
Flowers, grass and trees,
Odor, grace and color:
Lovely gifts like these.

What makes a garden
And why do gardens grow?
Love lives in gardens —
God and lovers know.
            CAROLYN GILTINAN

THINGS THAT ARE FAMILIAR

Life has loveliness to sell,
All beautiful and splendid things,
Blue waves whitened on a cliff,
Soaring fire that sways and sings,
And children's faces looking up
Holding wonder like a cup.

Life has loveliness to sell,
Music like a curve of gold,
Scent of pine trees in the rain,
Eyes that love you, arms that hold,
And for your spirit's still delight,
Holy thoughts that star the night.

Spend all you have for loveliness,
Buy it and never count the cost;
For one whole singing hour of peace
Count many a year of strife well lost,
And for a breath of ecstasy
Give all you have been, or could be.

SARA TEASDALE

Night Magic

The apples falling from the tree
Make such a heavy bump at night
I always am surprised to see
They are so little, when it's light;

And all the dark just sings and sings
So loud, I cannot see at all
How frogs and crickets and such things
That make the noise, can be so small.

Then my own room looks larger, too —
Corners so dark and far away —
I wonder if things really do
Grow up at night and shrink by day?

AMELIA JOSEPHINE BURR

He blinks upon the hearth-rug
And yawns in deep content,
Accepting all the comforts
That Providence has sent.

Louder he purrs, and louder,
In one glad hymn of praise
For all the night's adventures,
For quiet, restful days.

Life will go on forever,
With all that cat can wish;
Warmth, and the glad procession
Of fish and milk and fish.

Only—the thought disturbs him—
He's noticed once or twice,
That times are somehow breeding
A nimbler race of mice.

              ALEXANDER GRAY

We sat together close and warm,
My little tired boy and I —
Watching across the evening sky
The coming of the storm.

No rumbling rose, no thunder crashed,
The west-wind scarcely sang aloud;
But from a huge and solid cloud
The summer lightnings flashed.

And then he whispered "Father, watch;
I think God's going to light His moon —"
"And when, my boy" ... "Oh, very soon.
I saw Him strike a match!"

              LOUIS UNTERMEYER

Old Homes! old hearts! Upon my Soul forever
Their peace and gladness lie like tears and laughter.

              MADISON CAWEIN

THINGS THAT ARE FAMILIAR

I walked among the tender grasses
    Sparkling in the dew,
I heard the whispering of the trees,
The morning call of birds, the murmer
    of the bees,
I watched the buds so quietly unfold
    to kiss the sun;
I felt the calm and gentle breeze when
    day is done,
And then I know
That God would walk and talk within
    my garden too.
                      GERTRUDE THOMPSON MILLER

    We who were born
    In country places
    Far from cities
    And shifting faces,
    We have a birthright
    No man can sell,
    And a secret joy
    No man can tell.
                EILUNED LEWIS

The Long Voyage

Not that the pines were darker there,
nor mid-May dogwood brighter there,
nor swifts more swift in summer air;
    it was my own country,

having its thunder-clap of spring,
its long midsummer ripening,
its corn hoar-stiff at harvesting,
    almost like any country,

yet being mine; its face, its speech,
its hills bent low within my reach,

its river birch and upland beech
   were mine, of my own country.
Now the dark waters at the bow
fold back, like earth against the plow;
foam brightens like the dogwood now
   at home, in my own country.

                  MALCOLM COWLEY

     Dark brown is the river,
     Golden is the sand.
     It flows along forever,
     With trees on either hand.

     Green leaves a-floating,
     Castles of the foam,
     Boats of mine a-boating —
     Where will all come home?

          ROBERT LOUIS STEVENSON

Why is it that the poets tell
So little of the sense of smell?
These are the odors I love well:

The smell of coffee freshly ground;
Or rich plum pudding, holly-crowned;
Or onions fried and deeply browned.

The fragrance of a fumy pipe;
The smell of apples, newly ripe;
And printer's ink on leaden type.

Woods by moonlight in September
Breathe most sweet; and I remember
Many a smoky campfire ember.

Camphor, turpentine, and tea,
The balsam of a Christmas tree,
These are whiffs of gramarye . . .
A ship smells best of all to me!

              CHRISTOPHER MORLEY

THINGS THAT ARE FAMILIAR

MEMORIES THROUGH THE YEAR

Memories are symphonies — music of the years,
Lifting us to praises, casting out our fears;
Warming our affections, driving away pain,
Sweetening the bitter cup, bringing joy again.
Memories are flowers that can never fade,
That we all have nurtured, in sunshine, and in shade;
Garden of the Spirit, Mind, and Heart and Life —
Giving fragrance all around where is care and strife.
Memories are pictures, with their colors bright,
With their lights and shadows, as our "day and night."

METTA WRIGHT

Memory is the bridge that spans the gulf of time.
It is built of smiles and tears,
It is built of hopes and fears,
And its length is years and years —
Some of joy and some are drear,
But to all of us most dear
   Is Memory.

ANNE WOOD

Old Summers

I sing a song of old summers;
A song as old as the sea.
I sing a song that is not a song;
Just something for you and me.

Something so wistful and splendid,
Something so loving and true;
It seems that my fault is mended
Back with old summers and you.

Faces that form in the embers,
Ones that we loved in review,
Smiling, I see she remembers
Back to those summers and you.

EDWARD FLORENCE

My favorite dress
I must confess
Is not my red or blue or pink
(They're fine, I think)
But I like climbing trees and walls —
My favorite dress is overalls!
My favorite hat has nothing on it;
It's just my everyday sunbonnet.
My favorite summer shoes, you say?
Ha! I go barefoot all the day!

MATTIE LEE HAUSGEN

Four ducks on a pond,
A grass-bank beyond,
A blue sky of spring,
White clouds on the wing —
What a little thing
To remember for years!
To remember with tears!
    WILLIAM ALLINGHAM

Now has the blue-eyed Spring
Sped dancing through the plain.
Girls weave a daisy chain;
Boys race beside the sedge;
Dust fills the blinding lane;
May lies upon the hedge;
All creatures love Spring!

The clouds laugh on, and would
Dance with us if they could;
The larks ascend and shrill;
A woodpecker fills the wood;
Jays laugh crossing the hill;
All creatures love the Spring!

The lithe cloud-shadows chase
Over the whole earth's face,
And where winds ruffling veer
O'er wooded streams dark ways
Mad fish unscudding steer;
All creatures love the Spring!

Run, girls, to drink thick cream!
Race, boys, to where the stream
Winds through a rumbling pool,
And your bright bodies fling
Into the foaming cool!
For we'll enjoy our Spring!
    ROBERT NICHOLS

The wind is sewing with needles of rain;
With shining needles of rain
It stitches into the thin
Cloth of earth — in,
In, in, in,

Oh, the wind has often sewed with me! —
One, two, three.

Spring must have fine things
To wear, like other springs.
Of silken green the grass must be
Embroidered. One and two and three.

Then every crocus must be made
So subtly as to seem afraid
Of lifting color from the ground;
And after crocuses, the round
Heads of tulips and all the fair
Intricate garb that Spring will wear.
The wind must sew with needles of rain,
With shining needles of rain
Stitching into the thin
Cloth of earth — in,
In, in, in —

For all the springs of futurity.
One, two, three.

                              HAZEL HALL

The year's at the spring,
And day's at the morn;
Morning's at seven;
The hillside's dew-pearled;
The lark's on the wing;
The snail's on the thorn;
God's in his heaven —
All's right with the world.
                ROBERT BROWNING

And lilac, loveliest as I walk
At evening time
Along the road that brings me to my home
               HENRY TREECE

    Love and laughing youth
    And a rain-washed spring:
    These are truth
    And a memorable thing.
               CHARLES KENNEDY

Raining, raining,
All night long;
Sometimes loud, sometimes soft,
Just like a song.

There'll be rivers in the gutters
And lakes along the street.
It will make our lazy kitty
Wash his little dirty feet.

The roses will wear diamonds
Like kings and queens at court;
But the pansies all get muddy
Because they are so short.

I'll sail my boat tomorrow
In wonderful new places,
But first I'll take my watering-pot
And wash the pansies' faces.
               AMELIA JOSEPHINE BURR

This memory brightens o'er the past,
As when the sun, concealed
Behind some cloud that near us hangs,
Shines on a distant field.
               HENRY WADSWORTH LONGFELLOW

MEMORIES THROUGH THE YEAR

Hallowe'en

Tonight is the night
When dead leaves fly
Like witches on switches
Across the sky,
When elf and sprite
Flit through the night
On a moony sheen.

Tonight is the night
When leaves make a sound
Like a gnome in his home
Under the ground,
When spooks and trolls
Creep out of holes
Mossy and green.

Tonight is the night
When pumpkins stare
Through sheaves and leaves
Everywhere,
When ghoul and ghost
And goblin host
Dance round their queen.
It's Hallowe'en.

     HARRY BEHN

I like the fall,
The mist and all.
I like the night owl's
Lonely call —
And wailing sound
Of wind around.

I like the gray
November day,
And bare, dead boughs
That coldly sway

Against my pane.
I like the rain.

I like to sit
And laugh at it —
And tend
My cozy fire a bit.
I like the fall —
The mist and all. —
   DIXIE WILLSON

First, April, she with mellow showers
Opens the way for early flowers;
Then after her comes smiling May,
In a more sweet and rich array;
Next enters June, and brings us more
Gems than those two that went before;
Then, lastly, July comes and she
More wealth brings in than all those three.
   ROBERT HERRICK

Beech Leaves

In autumn down the beechwood path
The leaves lie thick upon the ground.
It's there I love to kick my way
And hear their crisp and crashing sound.

I am a giant, and my steps
Echo and thunder to the sky.
How the small creatures of the woods
Must quake and cower as I pass by!

This brave and merry noise I make
In summer also when I stride
Down to the shining, pebbly sea
And kick the frothing waves aside.
   JAMES REEVES

MEMORIES THROUGH THE YEAR

A frosty Christmas Eve
   when the stars were shining
Fared I forth alone
   where westward falls the hill,
And from many a village
   in the water'd valley
Distant music reach'd me
   peals of bells aringing:
The constellated sounds
   ran sprinkling on earth's floor
As the dark vault above
   with stars was spangled o'er.
ROBERT BRIDGES

Skating

When I try to skate,
My feet are so wary
They grit and they grate:
And then I watch Mary
Easily gliding,
Like an ice-fairy;
Skimming and curving,
Out and in,
With a turn of her head,
And a lift of her chin,
And a gleam of her eye,
And a twirl and a spin;
Sailing under
The breathless hush
Of the willows, and back
To the frozen mush;
Out to the island
And round the edge,
Skirting the rim
Of the crackling sedge,
Swerving close

To the poplar root,
And round the lake
On a single foot,
With a three, and an eight,
And a loop and a ring;
Where Mary glides,
The lake will sing!
Out in the mist
I hear her now
Under the frost
Of the willow-bough
Easily sailing,
Light and fleet,
With the song of the lake
Beneath her feet.

HERBERT ASQUITH

Dad always thought, and with some justification, that none of the professionals were as good a photographer as he. Consequently, when it came to taking pictures of the family, Dad liked to do the job himself.

He liked to do the job as often as possible, rain or shine, day or night, summer or winter, and especially on Sundays. Most photographers prefer sunlight for their pictures. But Dad liked it best when there was no sun and he had an excuse to take his pictures indoors. He seemed to have a special affinity for flashlight powder, and the bigger the flash the more he enjoyed it.

He'd pour great, gray mountains of the powder into the pan at the top of his T-shaped flash gun, and hold this as far over his head as possible with his left hand, while he burrowed beneath a black cloth at the stern of the camera. In his right hand, he'd hold the shutter release and a toy of some kind, which he'd shake and rattle to get our attention.

Probably few men have walked away from larger flash-

MEMORIES THROUGH THE YEAR

light explosions than those Dad set off as a matter of routine. The ceilings of some of the rooms in Montclair bore charred, black circles, in mute testimony to his intrepidity as an exploder. Some of the professional photographers, seeing him load a flash gun, would blanch, mutter, and hasten from the room.

"I know what I'm doing," Dad would shout after them irritably. "Go ahead, then, if you don't want to learn anything. But when I'm through, just compare the finished product with the kind of work you do."

The older children had been through it so often that, while somewhat shellshocked, they were no longer terrified. It would be stretching a point to say they had developed any real confidence in Dad's indoor photography. But at least they had adopted a fatalistic attitude that death, if it came, would be swift and painless. The younger children, unfortunately, had no such comforting philosophy to fall back on. They'd behave pretty well right up to the time Dad was going to take the picture. Then they'd start bellowing.

"Lillie, stop those children from crying," Dad would shout from under the black cloth. "Dan, open your eyes and take your fingers out of your ears! The idea! Scared of a little flash! And stop fidgeting, all of you."

He'd come up in disgust from under the cloth. It was hot under there, and the bending over had made the blood run to his head.

"Now stop crying, all of you," he'd say furiously. "Do you hear me? Next time I go under there I want to see all of you smiling."

He'd submerge again. "I said stop that crying. Now smile, or I'll come out and give you something to cry about. Smile so I can see the whites of your teeth. That's more like it."

He'd slip a plate holder into the back of the camera.

"Ready? Ready? Smile now. Hold it. Hold it. Hooold it."

He'd wave the toy furiously and then there'd be an

awful, blinding, roaring flash that shook the room and deposited a fine ash all over us and the floor. Dad would come up, sweaty but grinning. He'd look to see whether the ceiling was still there, and then put down the flash gun and go over and open the windows to let out a cloud of choking smoke that made your eyes water.

"I think that was a good picture," he'd say. "And this new flash gun certainly works fine. Don't go away now. I want to take one more as soon as the smoke clears. I'm not sure I had quite enough light that time."

FRANK B. GILBRETH, JR. and
ERNESTINE GILBRETH CAREY

Sing a song of winter,
Of frosty clouds in air!
Sing a song of snowflakes
Falling everywhere.

Sing a song of winter!
Sing a song of sleds!
Sing a song of tumbling
Over heels and heads.

Up and down a hillside
When the moon is bright,
Sledding is a tiptop
Wintertime delight.

NORMAN C. SCHLICHTER

The morns are meeker than they were,
The nuts are getting brown;
The berry's cheek is plumper,
The rose is out of town.

The maple wears a gayer scarf,
The field a scarlet gown.
Lest I should be old-fashioned,
I'll put a trinket on.

EMILY DICKINSON

MEMORIES THROUGH THE YEAR

And what is so rare as a day in June?
Then, if ever, come perfect days;
Then Heaven tries earth if it be in tune,
And over it softly her warm ear lays:
Whether we look, or whether we listen,
We hear life murmur, or see it glisten;
Every clod feels a stir of might,
An instinct within it that reaches and towers,
And, groping blindly above it for light,
Climbs to a soul in grass and flowers;
The flush of life may well be seen
Thrilling back over hills and valleys;
The cowslip startles in meadows green,
The buttercup catches the sun in its chalice,

And there's never a leaf nor a blade too mean
To be some happy creature's palace;
The little bird sits at his door in the sun,
Atilt like a blossom among the leaves,
And lets his illumined being o'errun
With the deluge of summer it receives;
His mate feels the eggs beneath her wings,
And the heart in her dumb breast flutters and sings;
He sings to the wide world, and she to her nest,
In the nice ear of Nature which song is best?

JAMES RUSSELL LOWELL

I'm wishing the whole world Christmas —
The children, the beasts, and the birds;
I'm wishing the whole world Christmas —
And I'd like to have magical words
To wish just the shining wish I would wish
In the Christmas words I would say,
For I'm wishing the whole world Christmas,
And joy on Christmas Day.

O, I'd need a pen to write golden,
The goldenest pen indeed,

To wish the whole world Christmas
For the happy children to read.
I'm wishing the whole world Christmas
And may the dear Lord be kind,
And send blessings down like snowflakes
For all of His children to find . . .

       ANNETTE WYNNE

Village Christmas

As I went down the village street
The wind blew glittering and light
And one last church-bell quivered sweet
And wreath-hung doors stood kind and bright

And past the hedge-lines' ruffs of snow
As by each little house I came
Like rosy tulip-buds arow
I saw the window candles flame.

And round a silver shining tree
Between the starlight and the snow
Our children all sang merrily
How Christ and joy were here below:

And Christ was there and joy was there:
Still we could love, and still believe.
I bent my head and said my prayer;
"I thank You, Lord, for Christmas Eve."

       MARGARET WIDDEMER

  When Time who steals our years away
  Shall steal our pleasures too,
  The mem'ry of the past will stay,
  And half our joys renew.

       THOMAS MOORE

MEMORIES THROUGH THE YEAR

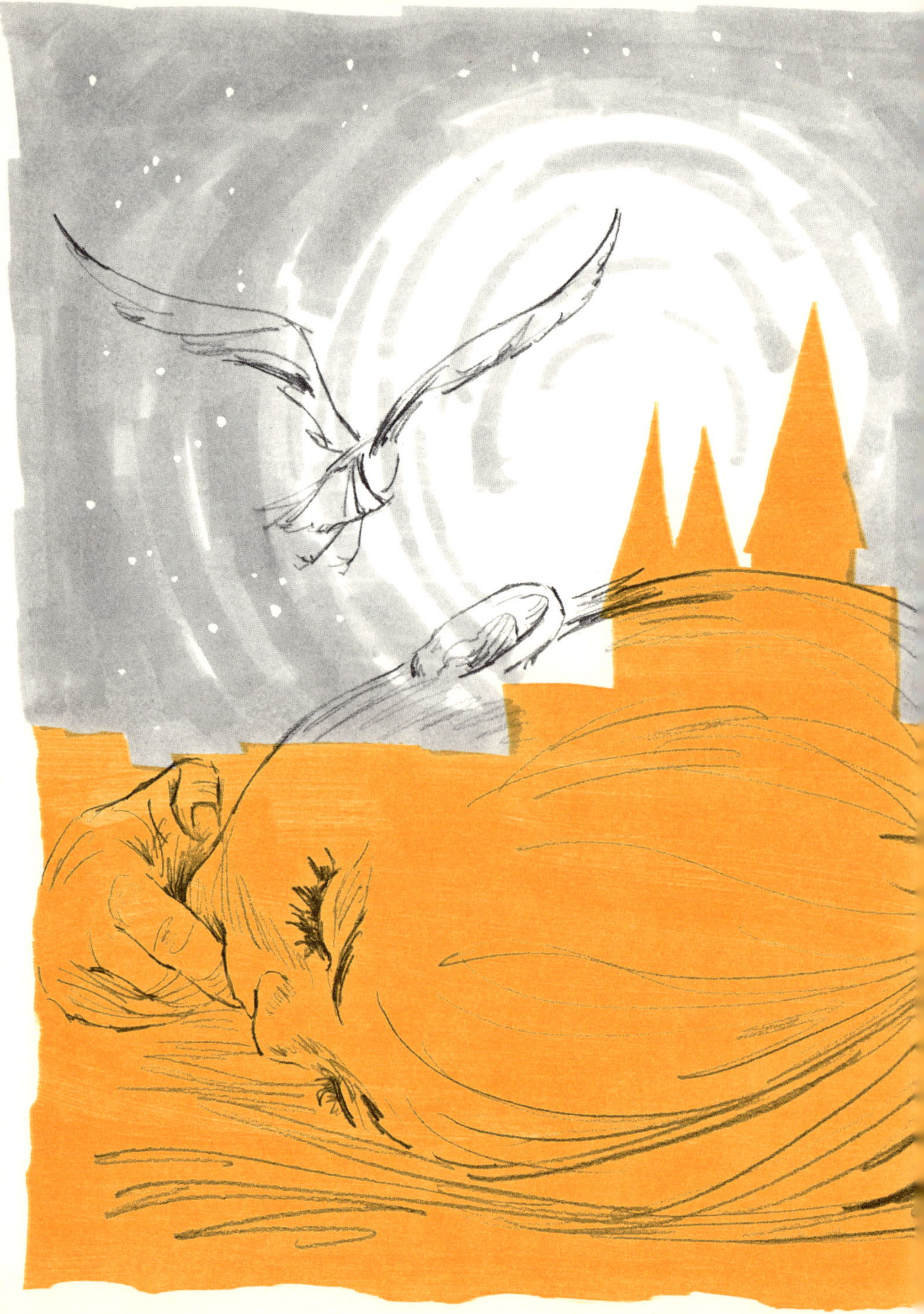

SWEET DREAMS

Dream happy dreams, my dear,
And dream good dreams,
That peace and patience teach;
Dream noble dreams, magic dreams,
And lofty dreams
That far out span your earthly reach.

What if your dreams are broken
On life's surging wheel?
What if each shattered dream
New disillusion brings?
When from the broken strands
Of childhood dreams
Are woven vast, accomplished things.

OMA CARLYLE ANDERSON

The lights from the parlor and kitchen shone out
Through the blinds and the windows and bars;
And high overhead and all moving about,
There were thousands of millions of stars.
There ne'er were such thousands of leaves on a tree,
Nor of people in church or the Park,
As the crowds of the stars that looked down upon me,
And that glittered and winked in the dark.

The Dog, and the Plough, and the Hunter, and all,
And the star of the sailor, and Mars,
These shone in the sky, and the pail by the wall
Would be half full of water and stars.
They saw me at last, and they chased me with cries,
And they soon had me packed into bed;
But the glory kept shining and bright in my eyes,
And the stars going round in my head.

       ROBERT LOUIS STEVENSON

I always liked to go to bed —
It looked so dear and white.
Besides, my mother used to tell
A story every night.

When other children cried to go
I did not mind at all,
She made such faery pageants grow
Upon the bedroom wall.

The room was full of slumber lights,
Of seas and ships and wings,
Of Holy Grails and swords and knights
And beautiful, kind kings.

And so she wove and wove and wove
Her singing thoughts through mine.
I heard them murmuring through my sleep,
Sweet, audible, and fine.

    ANNA HEMPSTEAD BRANCH

Daisies

At evening when I go to bed
I see the stars shine overhead;
They are the little daisies white
That dot the meadow of the night.

And often while I'm dreaming so,
Across the sky the moon will go;
It is a lady, sweet and fair,
Who comes to gather daisies there.

For, when at morning I arise,
There's not a star left in the skies;
She's picked them all and dropped them down
Into the meadows of the town.

            FRANK DEMPSTER SHERMAN

A Comparison

Apple blossoms look like snow,
They're different though,
Snow falls softly, but it brings
Noisy things:
Sleighs and bells, forts and fights,
Cosy nights.

But apple blossoms when they go,
White and slow,
Quiet all the orchard space,
Till the place
Hushed with falling sweetness seems
Filled with dreams.

            JOHN FARRAR

    When I could not sleep for cold,
    I had enough fire in my brain,
    And builded, with roofs of gold,
    My beautiful castles in Spain.
            JAMES RUSSELL LOWELL

SWEET DREAMS

Sunlight, moonlight,
Twilight, starlight —
Gloaming at the close of day,
And an owl calling,
Cool dews falling
In a wood of oak and may.

Lantern-light, taper-light,
Torch-light, no-light;
Darkness at the shut of day,
And lions roaring,
Their wrath pouring
In wild places far away.

Elf-light, bat-light,
Touchwood-light and toad-light,

And the sea a shimmering gloom of grey,
And a small face smiling
In a dream's beguiling
In a world of wonders far away.

                    WALTER DE LA MARE

Across the years he could recall
His father one way best of all.

In the stillest hour of night
The boy awakened to a light.

Half in dreams, he saw his sire
With his great hands full of fire.

The man had struck a match to see
If his son slept peacefully.

He held his palms each side the spark
His love had kindled in the dark.

His two hands were curved apart
In the semblance of a heart.

He wore, it seemed to his small son,
A bare heart on his hidden one,

A heart that gave out such a glow
No son awake could bear to know.

It showed a look upon a face
Too tender for the day to trace.

One instant, it lit all about,
And then secret heart went out.

But it shone long enough for one
To know that hands held up the sun.
        ROBERT P. TRISTRAM COFFIN

Yes, my darling, well I know
How the bitter wind doth blow;
And the winter's snow and rain
Patter on the window-pane:
But they cannot come in here,
To my little baby dear.

For the window shutteth fast,
Till the stormy night is past;
And the curtains warm are spread
Round about her cradle-bed:
So till morning shineth bright,
Little baby dear, goodnight.
        JANE TAYLOR

Wild Geese

I heard the wild geese flying
In the dead of the night,
With beats of wings and cry
I heard the wild geese flying.

And dreams in my heart sighing
Followed their northward flight.
I heard the wild geese flying
In the dead of the night.
        ELINOR CHIPP

At eventide, Oh Mother mine, when all is still,
The calm air undisturbed, except by night birds trill,
When setting sun has cast its glorious hues of rose
    and blue,

Then mem'ry comes, and peacefully we're drifting back
    to you.
At eventide I quit this busy thoroughfare,
Through years to you I fly, my love with you to share,
And oh, I see our dear old home, the rooms inviting,
    neat,
And in the old reed rocker sits my Mother, calm and
    sweet.

She sits and waits at eventide, she waits and dreams,
Of other days, 'twas only yesterday it seems,
And when we reach the place so dear, where she with
    loving care,
Had labored so unceasingly, how memory lingers there.

                        KATHRYN HAREN MEESTER

    So ends an autumn day,
    Light ripples on the ceiling,
    Dishes are stacked away;
    So ends an autumn day,
    The children jog and sway
    In comic dances wheeling.
    So ends an autumn day,
    Light ripples on the ceiling.

    They trail upstairs to bed,
    And night is a dark tower.
    The kettle calls: instead
    They trail upstairs to bed,
    Leaving warmth, the coppery-red
    Mood of their carnival hour.
    They trail upstairs to bed,
    And night is a dark tower.

                    BARBARA HOWES

I wandered lonely as a cloud
That floats on high o'er vales and hills,
When all at once I saw a crowd,
A host, of golden daffodils;
Beside the lake, beneath the trees,
Fluttering and dancing in the breeze.

Continuous as the stars that shine
And twinkle in the Milky Way,
They stretched in never-ending line
Along the margin of a bay:
Ten thousand saw I at a glance,
Tossing their heads in sprightly dance.

The waves beside them danced; but they
Outdid the sparkling waves in glee:
A poet could not but be gay
In such a jocund company:
I gazed — and gazed — but little thought
What wealth the show to me had brought:

For oft when on my couch I lie
In vacant or in pensive mood,
They flash upon that inward eye
Which is the bliss of solitude;
And then my heart with rapture fills,
And dances with the daffodils.

     WILLIAM WORDSWORTH

  Hold fast to dreams
  For if dreams die
  Life is a broken-winged bird
  That cannot fly.

  Hold fast to dreams
  For when dreams go
  Life is a barren field
  Frozen with snow.
     LANGSTON HUGHES

SWEET DREAMS

Tree Sleeping

When I was small and trees were high,
I loved to sleep out nights by the sea,
A spruce that held up half the sky
Had boughs like beds where I could lie,
So thick the twigs I could not slide
Through to earth, and at my side
The evening star lay close by me.

The night came over the ocean slow,
A wind came up from nowhere there,
I felt my tree go to and fro
Until my bed was wholly air,
I lay on music grave and deep,
Moved on oceans of holy sleep,
With great stars tangled in my hair.

A sea-bird on a snowy wing
Came down with treble cries,
Alighted on my bed, this thing
Woke me with wide surprise,
Flew off with golden talons curled,
And there on the blue edge of the world
The young sun looked me in the eyes.

ROBERT P. TRISTRAM COFFIN

Hold fast your dreams!
Within your heart,
Keep one still secret spot
Where dreams may go,
And sheltered so,
May thrive and grow —
Where doubt and fear are not.
Oh, keep a place apart
Within your heart,
For little dreams to go.

LOUISE DRISCOLL

Five minutes, five minutes more, please!
Let me stay five minutes more!
Can't I just finish the castle
I'm building here on the floor?
Can't I just finish the story
I'm reading here in my book?
Can't I just finish this bead-chain —
It almost is finished, look!
Can't I just finish this game, please?
When a game's once begun
It's a pity never to find out
Whether you've lost or won.
Can't I just stay five minutes?
Well, can't I stay just four?
Three minutes, then? two minutes?
Can't I stay one minute more?

      ELEANOR FARJEON

Be Not Afraid

Be not afraid because the sun goes down;
It brings the sunset and the plover's cry.
Before the colors of the evening drown,
The stars will make new colors in the sky.
Night is no enemy. She passes by,
And shows us silence for our own heart's good;
For while we sleep, the roses multiply,
The little tree grows taller in the wood.
Fear not the night; the morning follows soon.
Each has his task to make the earth more fair.
It is by these, by midnight and by noon,
That she grows riper and her orchards bear.
Her fields would wither in a sun too bright;
They need the darknesss too. Fear not the night.

      ROBERT NATHAN

SWEET DREAMS

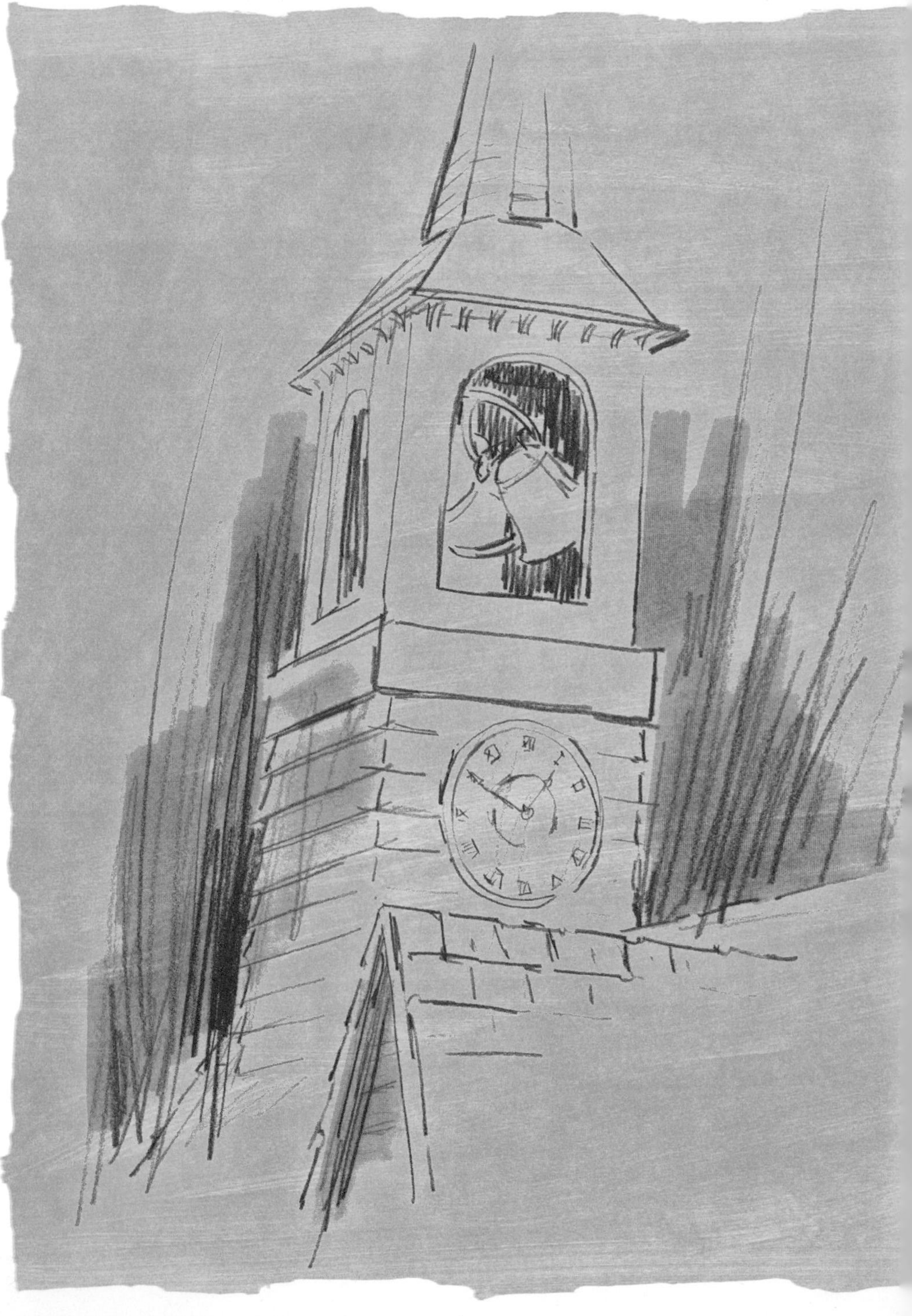

ECHOES THAT REMAIN

V

O there are Voices of the Past,
Links of a broken chain,
Wings that can bear me back to Times
Which cannot come again;
Yet God forbid that I should lose
The echoes that remain.

ADELAIDE ANN PROCTER

Piano

Softly, in the dusk, a woman is singing
   to me;
Taking me back with the vista of years,
   till I see
A child sitting under the piano, in the
   boom of the tingling strings
And pressing the small, poised feet of a
   mother who smiles as she sings.

In spite of myself, the insidious mastery
   of song
Betrays me back, till the heart of me
   weeps to belong
To the old Sunday evenings at home, with
   the winter outside
And hymns in the cozy parlor, the tinkling
   piano our guide.

                        D. H. LAWRENCE

    I have loved flowers that fade,
    Within whose magic tents
    Rich hues have marriage made
    With sweet unmemoried scents:
    A honeymoon delight,—
    A joy of love at sight,
    That ages in an hour:—
    My song be like a flower!

                    ROBERT BRIDGES

    I heard the bells on Christmas Day
    Their old, familiar carols play,
    And wild and sweet
    The words repeat
    Of peace on earth, good-will to men!

         HENRY WADSWORTH LONGFELLOW

Once as I travelled through a quiet evening,
I saw a pool, jet-black and mirror still.
Beyond, the slender paperbacks stood crowding;
each on its own white image looked its fill,
and nothing moved but thirty egrets wading —
thirty egrets in a quiet evening.

Once in a lifetime, lovely past believing,
your lucky eyes may light on such a pool.
As though for many years I had been waiting,
I watched in silence, till my heart was full
of clear dark water, and white trees unmoving,
and, whiter yet, those egrets wading.

JUDITH WRIGHT

Voices

O there were lights and laughter
   And the motions to and fro
Of people as they enter
   And people as they go . . .

And there were many voices
   Vying at the feast,
But mostly I remember
   Yours — who spoke the least.

WITTER BYNNER

A picture memory brings to me:
I look across the years and see
Myself beside my mother's knee.

I feel her gentle hand restrain
My selfish moods, and know again
A child's blind sense of wrong and pain.

But wiser now, a man gray grown,
My childhood's needs are better known.
My mother's chastening love I own.

JOHN GREENLEAF WHITTIER

ECHOES THAT REMAIN

Memory

My mind lets go a thousand things
Like dates of wars and deaths of kings
And yet recalls the very hour —
'Twas noon by yonder village tower,
And on the last blue noon in May —
The wind came briskly up this way,
Crisping the brook beside the road;
Then, pausing here, set down its load
Of pine-scents, and shook listlessly
Two petals from that wild rose-tree.

    THOMAS BAILEY ALDRICH

Into my heart's treasury
I slipped a coin
That time cannot take
Nor thief purloin, —
Oh, better than minting
Of a gold-crowned king
Is the safe-kept memory
Of a lovely thing.

    SARA TEASDALE

"Dear little tree that we plant today,
What will you be when we're old and gray?"

"The savings bank of the squirrel and mouse,
For the robin and wren an apartment house;

The dressing room of the butterfly's ball;
The locust and katydid's concert hall;

The schoolboy's ladder in pleasant June,
The schoolgirl's tent in the July noon;

And my leaves shall whisper them merrily
A tale of the children who planted me."

    UNKNOWN

The sun does arise,
And make happy the skies;
The merry bells ring
To welcome the Spring;
The skylark and the thrush,
The birds of the bush,
Sing louder around
To the bells cheerful sound,
While our sports shall be seen
On the Echoing Green.

Old John, with white hair,
Does laugh away care,
Sitting under the oak,
Among the old folk,
They laugh at our play,
And soon they all say:
"Such, such were the joys
When we all, girls and boys,
In our youth time were seen
On the Echoing Green."

Till the little ones, weary,
No more can be merry;
The sun does descend,
And our sports have an end.
Round the laps of their mothers
Many sisters and brothers,
Like birds in their nest,
Are ready for rest,
And sport no more seen
On the darkening Green.

                    WILLIAM BLAKE

Things bygone are the only things that last:
The present is mere grass, quick-mown away;
The Past is stone, and stands forever fast.
              EUGENE LEE-HAMILTON

ECHOES THAT REMAIN

The birches that dance on the top of the hill
Are so slender and young that they cannot keep still,
They bend and they nod at each whiff of a breeze,
For you see they are still just the children of trees.
But the birches below in the valley are older,
They are calmer and straighter and taller and colder.
Perhaps when we've grown up as solemn and grave
We, too, will have children who do not behave!

JOHN FARRAR

To a Child with Eyes

Is there nothing left to see?
There is the squirrel. There is the bee.
There is the chipmunk on the wall,
And the first yellow of every fall.
There is the humming bird, the crow.
There is the lantern on the snow.
There is the new-appearing corn.
There is the colt a minute born . . .
Run and see, and say how many —
There are more if there is any!

MARK VAN DOREN

A Blackbird Suddenly

Heaven is in my hand, and I
Touch a heart-beat of the sky,
Hearing a blackbird's cry.

Strange, beautiful, unquiet thing,
Lone flute of God, how can you sing
Winter to spring?

You have outdistanced every voice and word,
And given my spirit wings until it stirred
Like you — a bird!

JOSEPH AUSLANDER

Scraps

The loves I knew are like old garments now.
They're faded and like ordinary clothes
Have lost the charm and brightness they possessed
When they were fresh and new and in demand.
But I have kept a sample from each one
When it was new, in bags of memories.
Some day I'll take the little scrap-bags out
And piece a quilt from all the bits of love.
I'll make a striking pattern, passion-reds
All strewn like flowers, mixed with friendship blues.
I'll stitch them all together with a thread
Of recollection. When the sun of youth
Has set and middle-life's dim twilight warns
The night of age is near, I shall not be
One huddled up, afraid, for I shall have
My coverlet of love to keep me warm.

GLADYS PUGH

The childhood shows the man
As morning shows the day.

JOHN MILTON

I walk upon the rocky shore,
Her strength is in the ocean's roar.
I glance into the shaded pool,
Her mind is there so calm and cool.
I hear sweet rippling of the sea,
Naught but her laughter 'tis to me.
I gaze into the starry skies,
And there I see her wondrous eyes.
I look into my inmost mind,
And here her inspiration find.
In all I am and hear and see,
My precious mother is to me.

JOSEPHINE RICE CREELMAN

Often I think of the days long ago
When only a boy, I ran to and fro
Over fields and hills of the old home place,
And think of the boys who joined in the chase.

As plain to me now as they were right then
The boys of that age which are now old men,
And the ivy which grew there on the wall
With evergreen leaves through winter and fall.

I think again of the moss-covered trees.
That bend to and fro with the blowing breeze,
The dearest old spot to me ever made,
Underneath those trees where we youngsters played.

Many years have passed and have gone their way
But I still remember that youthful day,
With the things that made living there so dear,
And that which grows sweeter each passing year.

But the dear old homestead has long since gone,
Even the building in which I was born,
Yet its memory will always remain
When I think of those trees there in the lane.

JESSE J. GOULD

To think I once saw grocery shops
With but a casual eye
And fingered figs and apricots
As one who came to buy!

To think I never dreamed of how
Bananas swayed in rain,
And often looked at oranges
Yet never thought of Spain!

And in those wasted days I saw
No sails above the tea —
For grocery shops were grocery shops,
Not hemispheres to me!

ELIZABETH COATSWORTH

My heart leaps up when I behold
A rainbow in the sky.
So was it when my life began;
So is it now I am a man.
                WILLIAM WORDSWORTH

The summer is over,
The trees are bare,
There is mist on the garden
And frost in the air.
The meadows are empty
And gathered the sheaves —
But isn't it lovely
Kicking up leaves!

John from the garden
Has taken the chairs;
It's dark in the evening
And cold on the stairs.
Winter is coming
And everyone grieves —
But isn't it lovely
Kicking up leaves!
                ROSE FYLEMAN

There is a difference between doing nothing and being bored. Being bored is a judgment you make on yourself. Doing nothing is a state of being.

Kids know about this, if you'll leave them be.
                ROBERT PAUL SMITH

Hors d'oeuvres have always a pathetic interest for me: they remind me of one's childhood that one goes through, wondering what the next course is going to be like — and during the rest of the menu one wishes one had eaten more of the hors d'oeuvres.
                SAKI

ECHOES THAT REMAIN

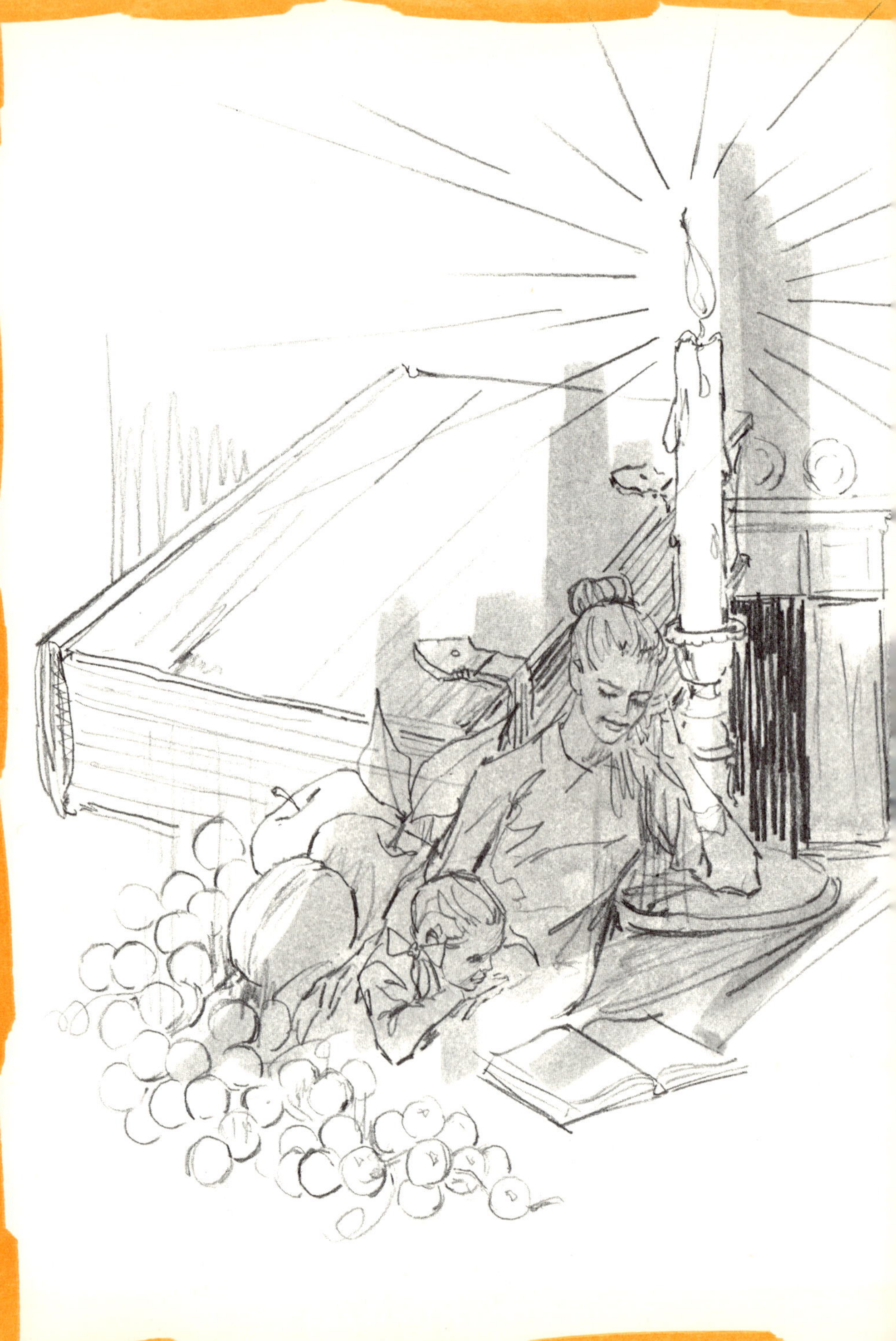

THE HEARTH OF HOME

> But what on earth is half so dear —
> So longed for — as the hearth of home?
> EMILY BRONTE

VI

All day I did the little things,
The little things that do not show;
I brought the kindling for the fire
I set the candles in a row,
I filled a bowl with marigolds,
The shallow bowl you love the best —
And made the house a pleasant place
Where weariness might take its rest.

The hours sped on, my eager feet
Could not keep pace with my desire.
So much to do, so little time!
I could not let my body tire;
Yet, when the coming of the night
Blotted the garden from my sight,
And on the narrow, graveled walks
Between the guarding flower stalks
I heard your step: I was not through
With services I meant for you.

You came into the quiet room
That glowed enchanted with the bloom
Of yellow flame. I saw your face,
Illumined by the firelit space,
Slowly grow still and comforted —
"It's good to be at home," you said.

BLANCHE BANE KUDER

Who loves the rain
And loves his home,
And looks on life with quiet eyes,
Him will I follow through the storm;
And at his hearth-fire keep me warm;
Nor hell nor heaven shall that soul surprise
Who loves the rain,
And loves his home,
And looks on life with quiet eyes.

FRANCES SHAW

I search among the plain and lovely words
To find what the one word "Mother" means; as well
Try to define the tangled song of birds;
The echo in the hills of one clear bell.
One cannot snare the wind, or catch the wings
Of shadows flying low across the wheat;
Ah, who can prison simple, natural things
That make the long days beautiful and sweet?

"Mother" — a word that holds the tender spell
Of all the dear essential things of earth;
A home, clean sunlit rooms, and the good smell
Of bread; a table spread; a glowing hearth.

And love beyond the dream of anyone . . .
I search for words for her . . . and there are
   none.
GRACE NOLL CROWELL

You may have tangible wealth untold;
Caskets of jewels and coffers of gold.
Richer than I you can never be —
I had a Mother who read to me.
STRICKLAND GILLILAN

God made a wonderful mother,
A mother who never grows old;
He made her smile of the sunshine,
And He molded her heart of pure gold;
In her eyes he placed bright shining stars,
In her cheeks, fair roses you see;
God made a wonderful mother,
And He gave that dear mother to me.
PAT O'REILLY

Happiness grows at our own firesides, and is not to be picked up in strangers' gardens.
DOUGLAS JERROLD

THE HEARTH OF HOME

To Adam paradise was home. To the good among his descendants home is paradise.

UNKNOWN

My Prairies

I love my prairies, they are mine
From zenith to horizon line,
Clipping a world of sky and sod
Like the bended arm and wrist of God.

I love their grasses. The skies
Are larger, and my restless eyes
Fasten on more of earth and air
Than seashore furnishes anywhere.

I love the hazel thickets; and the breeze,
The never resting prairie winds. The trees
That stand like spear points high
Against the dark blue sky

Are wonderful to me. I love the gold
Of newly shaven stubble, rolled
A royal carpet toward the sun, fit to be
The pathway of a deity.

I love the life of pasture lands; the song of birds
Are not more thrilling to me than the herd's
Mad bellowing or the shadow stride
Of mounted herdsmen at my side.

I love my prairies, they are mine
From high sun to horizon line.
The mountains and the cold gray sea
Are not for me, are not for me.

HAMLIN GARLAND

Yes, heaven is everywhere at home,
The big blue cap that always fits.

GILBERT KEITH CHESTERTON

When home is ruled according to God's word, angels might be asked to stay with us, and they would not find themselves out of their element.

CHARLES SPURGEON

Home's not merely four square walls,
Though with pictures hung and gilded;
Home is where Affection calls —
Filled with shrines the Hearth had builded!
Home! Go watch the faithful dove,
Sailing 'neath the heaven above us,
Home is where there is one to love!
Home's not merely roof and room,
It needs something to endear it;
Home is where the heart can bloom,
Where there's some kind lip to cheer it!
What is home with none to meet,
None to welcome, none to greet us?
Home is sweet, and only sweet,
Where there's one we love to meet us!

CHARLES SWAIN

Dear little house, dear shabby street,
Dear books and beds and food to eat,
How feeble words are to express
The facets of your tenderness.

How white the sun comes through the pane!
In tinkling music drips the rain!
How burning bright the furnace glows!
What paths to shovel when it snows!

Let these poor rhymes abide for proof
Joy dwells beneath a humble roof;
Heaven is not built of country seats
But little queer suburban streets!

CHRISTOPHER MORLEY

THE HEARTH OF HOME

Just a little shingle roof
Held up by four square walls,
Flooded inside with smiles of sunshine
And happiness enthralls.
No costly pictures adorn the walls,
No divans cushioned seat;
But above all this I value more
Love and home so sweet.

                        EFFIE CLOUSE

I wish, how I wish, that I had a little house,
With a mat for the cat and a hole for a mouse,
And a clock going "tock" in a corner of the room
And a kettle, and a cupboard, and a big birch broom.

To school in the morning the children off would run,
And I'd give them a kiss and a penny and a bun.
But directly they had gone from this little house
   of mine,
I'd clasp my hands and snatch a cloth, and shine,
   shine, shine.

I'd shine all the knives, all the windows and
   the floors
All the grates, all the plates, all the handles
   on the doors,
Every fork, every spoon, every lid, and every tin,
Till everything was shining like a new bright pin.

At night, by the fire, when the children were in bed,
I'd sit and I'd knit, with a cap upon my head,
And the kettles, and the saucepans they would shine,
   shine, shine,
In this tweeny little, cosy little house of mine!

                        NANCY M. HAYES

His home, the spot of earth supremely blest,
A dearer sweeter spot than all the rest.

                        UNKNOWN

Lord, behold our family here assembled. We thank Thee for this place in which we dwell; for the love that unites us; for the peace accorded us this day; for the hope with which we expect tomorrow; for the health, the work, the food, and the bright skies that make our lives delightful; for our friends in all parts of the world.

A FAMILY PRAYER

I have the most exacting little house;
It orders curtains made with fluted frills
And bids me loop them back with colored ties,
And grow geraniums for its window sills.

It even had me plant a lilac tree,
Where it could sniff the fragrance in the spring,
And now it wants a yellow jasmine vine:
I wonder what will be the next new thing!

When I come home, if only gone an hour,
It holds out eager arms to gather me
Within its door again — and then perhaps
It wants to ask a neighbor in to tea.

I may demur and argue for a time,
But in the end I let it have its way,
Because at night when everything is still,
It holds me close and listens while I pray.

HAZEL HARPER HARRIS

I see from my house by the side of the road
   By the side of the highway of life,
The men who press with the ardor of hope,
   The men who are faint with the strife,
But I turn not away from their smiles and their tears,
   Both parts of an infinite plan —
Let me live in a house by the side of the road
   And be a friend to man.

SAM WALTER FOSS

THE HEARTH OF HOME

Who's In

"The door is shut fast
And everyone's out."
But people don't know
What they are talking about!

Says the fly on the wall,
And the flame on the coals,
And the dog on his rug,
And the mice in their holes,
And the kitten curled up,
And the spiders that spin —
"What, everyone out?
Why, everyone's in!"

ELIZABETH FLEMING

Song for a Little House

I'm glad our house is a little house,
   Not too tall nor too wide:
I'm glad the hovering butterflies
   Feel free to come inside.

Our little house is a friendly house,
   It is not shy or vain;
It gossips with the talking trees,
   And makes friends with the rain.

And quick leaves cast a shimmer of green
   Against our whited walls,
And in the phlox, the courteous bees
   Are paying duty calls.

CHRISTOPHER MORLEY

Christianity begins at home. We build our character there, and what we become in after years is largely determined by our training and home environment.

TILLMAN HOBSON

A home is the place where folks are supreme,
The place to delight in, a glorified dream,
Where love is the guest, like a beautiful queen,
And Peace weaves a charm for the tranquilest scene.

HOWARD PHILIPS

Days Long Past

Oh! Long and long and long ago
We roamed the woodlands paths together;
Hand in hand we climbed the hills
To greet the newly risen sun;
We watched the maples clothe themselves
In veils of misty living red;
We searched the dark and leafy mould
To find the shyest hidden flowers,
And stood entranced at dogwood trees
Aglow beneath new forest leaves.
Today, you walk the hills alone;
I cook and wash and mend, to keep
For you and them this quiet place
Within four closing walls, called home:
But yesterday you brought to me
A spray of fragile Arbutus
Evoking tender memories
Of youthful days long past and gone.

MABEL C. B. MILLEN

Whom God loves, his house is sweet to him.

CERVANTES

Peace and rest at length have come,
All the day's long toil is past;
And each heart is whispering "Home,
Home at last!"

THOMAS HOOD

THE HEARTH OF HOME

Bells in the country,
They sing the heart to rest
When night is on the high road
And day is in the west.

And once they came to my house
As soft as beggars shod,
And brought it nearer heaven,
And maybe nearer God.

ROBERT NATHAN

A Prayer for a Little Home

God send us a little home,
To come back to, when we roam.

Low walls and fluted tiles,
Wide windows, a view for miles.

Red firelight and deep chairs,
Small white beds upstairs —

Great talk in little nooks,
Dim colors, rows of books.

One picture on each wall,
Not many things at all.

God send us a little ground,
Tall trees stand round.

Homely flowers in brown sod,
Overhead, thy stars, O God.

God bless thee, when winds blow,
Our home, and all we know.

FLORENCE BONE

Where we love is home,
Home that our feet may leave,
but not our hearts.

OLIVER WENDELL HOLMES

This be the verse you grave for me:
Here he lies where he longed to be,
Home is the sailor, home from the sea,
And the hunter home from the hill.
     ROBERT LOUIS STEVENSON

Nor has the world a better thing,
Though one should search it round,
Than thus to live one's own sole king,
Upon one's own sole ground.
     WILFRED BLUNT

But every house where Love abides
And Friendship is a guest,
Is surely home, and home sweet home,
For there the heart can rest.
     HENRY VAN DYKE

Stay, stay at home, my heart, and rest;
Home-keeping hearts are happiest,
For those that wander they know not where
Are full of trouble and full of care;
To stay at home is best.
     HENRY WADSWORTH LONGFELLOW

For mother-love and father-care,
For brothers strong and sisters fair,
For love at home and here each day,
For guidance lest we go astray,
Father in Heaven, we thank Thee.

For this new morning with its light,
For rest and shelter of the night,
For health and food, for love and friends,
For everything His goodness sends,
Father in Heaven, we thank Thee.
     CHRISTOPHER MORLEY

THE HEARTH OF HOME

Oh! mystery of man, from what a depth
Proceed thy honors. I am lost, but see
In simple childhood something of the base
On which thy greatness stands.

                        WILLIAM WORDSWORTH

Mid pleasures and palaces though we may roam,
Be it ever so humble, there's no place like
   home;
A charm from the sky seems to hallow us there,
Which, seek through the world, is ne'er met
   with elsewhere.
Home, home, sweet, sweet home!
There's no place like home! There's no place
   like home!

                        JOHN HOWARD PAYNE

Old Log House

On a little green knoll
At the edge of the wood
My great great grandmother's
First house stood.

The house was of logs
My grandmother said
With one big room
And a lean-to shed.

The logs were cut
And the house was raised
By pioneer men
In the olden days.

I like to hear
My grandmother tell
How they built the fireplace
And dug the well.

They split the shingles;
They filled each chink;
It's a house of which
I like to think.

Forever and ever
I wish I could
Live in a house
At the edge of a wood.
JAMES S. TIPPETT

Cleave to thine acre; the round year
Will fetch all fruits and virtues here.
Fool and foe may harmless roam,
Loved and lovers bide at home.
RALPH WALDO EMERSON

These have I loved
    White plates and cups, clean-gleaming,
Ringed with blue lines; and feathery faery dust:
Wet roofs, beneath the lamp-light; the strong crust
Of friendly bread; and many-tasting food;
Rainbows; and the blue bitter smoke of wood;
And radiant raindrops couching in cool flowers;
And flowers themselves, that sway through sunny hours,
Dreaming of moths that drink them under the moon;
Then, the cool kindliness of sheets, that soon
Smooth away trouble; and the rough male kiss
Of blankets; grainy wood; live hair that is
Shining and free; blue-massing clouds; the keen
Unpassioned beauty of a great machine;
The benison of hot water; furs to touch;
The good smell of old clothes; and other such —
The comfortable smell of friendly fingers,
Hair's fragrance, and the musty reek that lingers
About dead leaves and last year's ferns. . . .
RUPERT BROOKE

THE HEARTH OF HOME

A Prayer for Thanksgiving

We thank thee for our daily bread,
For faith by which the soul is fed,
For burdens given us to bear,
For hope that lifts the heart's despair.

We thank thee, Lord, for eyes to see
The truth that makes, and keeps, men free;
For faults — and the strength to mend them,
For dreams — and courage to defend them.

We have so much to thank thee for,
Dear Lord, we beg but one boon more;
Peace in the hearts of all men living,
Peace in the whole world this Thanksgiving.
      JOSEPH AUSLANDER

Through all the frozen winter
My nose has grown most lonely
For lovely, lovely, colored smells
That come in springtime only.

The purple smell of lilacs,
The yellow smell that blows
Across the air of meadows
Where bright forsythia grows.

The tall pink smell of peach trees,
The low white smell of clover,
And everywhere the great green smell
Of grass the whole world over.
      KATHRYN WORTH

Sweet white clover
Brings to me
Carefree days
Of infancy.
  JOSEPHINE JOHNSON

Cold winter now is in the wood,
The moon wades deep in snow.
Pile balsam boughs about the sills,
And let the fires glow!

The cows must stand in the dark barn,
The horses stamp all day.
Now shall the housewife bake her pies
And keep her kitchen gay.

The cat sleeps warm beneath the stove,
The dog on paws outspread;
But the brown deer with flinching hide
Seeks for a sheltered bed.

The fox steps hungry through the brush,
The lean hawk coasts the sky.
"Winter is in the wood!" the winds
In the warm chimney cry.

     ELIZABETH COATSWORTH

Grandma's kitchen was a special place,
Cheery, warm and bright,
Where the sun would softly touch the walls
With its first gentle light.

But even before sun-up,
Grandma was always there —
The delicious aroma of baking
Filling the morning air.

And when I smelled those cookies
I'd be up and on the run
To the kitchen for a sample
Of the first batch that was done.

There are many happy memories
Pleasant to recall —
But Grandma in her kitchen
Is the dearest one of all.

     MARY HURLEY

THE HEARTH OF HOME

She sits in the parlor a-dreaming;
Her face wears a radiant smile;
Her eyes, although dimmed, yet are gleaming,
She's been reminiscing a while.

She says she likes this quiet spot,
When twilight descends on the world.
Then the cares of life are soon forgot
And memories through her head swirl.

We thought she had taken her knitting.
Ah, yes! There it is in her lap.
But mem'ries have been her undoing,
Since she's had her little "cat-nap".

We know she's gone back to olden days,
With grandfather close by her side;
For her face shows in so many ways
Her love for him; also her pride.

Hush! There's no cause to let her suspect
That we have been peeping. For when
We light the candles, her thoughts'll be checked;
She'll pick up her knitting again.

RUTH EMILIE MILLER

Those evening bells! those evening bells!
How many a tale their music tells,
Of youth, and home, and that sweet time
When last I heard their soothing chime.

THOMAS MOORE

Acknowledgments

The editor and the publisher have made every effort to trace the ownership of all copyrighted material and to secure permission from holders of such material. In the event of any question arising as to the use of any material the publisher and editor, while expressing regret for inadvertent error, will be pleased to make the necessary corrections in future printings. Thanks are due to the following authors, publishers, publications and agents for permission to use the material indicated.

Angus & Robertson Ltd. and The Society of Authors for "Egrets" from *Birds* by Judith Wright.

Elizabeth Coatsworth Beston, for "April Fool" by Elizabeth Coatsworth from *The Reading of Poetry* by William Sheldon, Nellie Lyons and Polly Rovalt, published by Allyn and Bacon 1965.

Hazel Harris Brandner, for "My Little House" from *Winds of the Morning* by Hazel Harris, copyright by Hazel Harris Brandner.

Association for Childhood Education International, for "The Shiny Little House" by Nancy M. Hayes, copyright 1962 by the Association.

The Clarendon Press, for "I Have Loved the Flowers that Fade" from *The Poetical Works of Robert Bridges*.

Miss D. E. Collins, for excerpt from *The Ballad of the White Horse* by G. K. Chesterton.

Coward-McCann, Inc., for "Counters" from *Compass Rose* by Elizabeth Coatsworth, copyright 1929 by Coward-McCann, Inc., renewed 1957 by Elizabeth Coatsworth.

Thomas Y. Crowell Company and William Heinemann Ltd., for excerpt from *Cheaper by the Dozen* by Frank B. Gilbreth, Jr., and Ernestine Gilbreth Carey, copyright 1948, 1963 by Frank B. Gilbreth, Jr. and Ernestine Gilbreth Carey.

Mary Carolyn Davies, for "Let's Have a Picnic Out-of-Doors."

Dodd, Mead & Company, Inc., for "The Great Lover" from *The Collected Poems of Rupert Brooke*, copyright 1915 by Dodd, Mead & Company, Inc., renewed 1943 by Edward Marsh; "Two Sewing" from *Curtains* by Hazel Hall, copyright 1921 by Ruth Hall.

Doubleday & Company, Inc., for "Village Christmas" from *The Dark Cavalier* by Margaret Widdemer, copyright 1958 by Margaret Widdemer; "October" from *Gay Go Up* by Rose Fyleman, copyright 1929, 1930, by Doubleday & Company, Inc.

Constance Garland Doyle and Isabel Garland Lord, for "My Prairies" by Hamlin Garland.

E. P. Dutton & Company, Inc., and William Heinemann Ltd., for "Beach Leaves" from *The Wandering Moon* by James Reeves, published 1960 by E. P. Dutton & Company, Inc.

Ann Elmo Agency, Inc., for "Lyric" from *Collected Poems of Henry Treece*.

Estate of Amelia J. B. Elmore, for "Night Magic" by Amelia Josephine Burr.

Rudolf Flesch, for thirteen quotations from *The New Book of Unusual Quotations*, copyright 1966 by Rudolf Flecsh.

Estate of Sir Alexander Gray, for "On a Cat Ageing" from *Gossip* by Alexander Gray.

Harcourt, Brace & World, Inc., for "The Secret Cavern" from *Little Girl and Boy Land* by Margaret Widdemer, copyright 1924 by Harcourt, Brace & World, Inc., renewed 1952 by Margaret Widdemer Schauffler; "Preludes" from *Collected Poems 1909-1962* by T. S. Eliot, copyright 1936 by Harcourt, Brace & World, Inc., renewed 1963, 1964 by T. S. Eliot; "Hallowe'en" from *The Little Hill* by Harry Behn, copyright 1949 by Harry Behn; "The Young Mystic" by Louis Untermeyer from *This Singing World* edited by Louis Untermeyer, copyright 1923 by Harcourt, Brace & World, Inc., renewed 1951 by Louis Untermeyer.

Harper & Row, Publishers, for excerpt from *Chips Off the Old Benchley* by Robert Benchley, copyright 1949 by Harper & Brothers; "Old Log House" from *A World To Know* by James S. Tippett, copyright 1933 by Harper & Brothers, renewed 1961 by Martha K. Tippett; "A Blackbird Suddenly" from *Sunrise Trumpets* by Joseph Auslander, copyright 1924 by Harper & Brothers, renewed 1952 by Joseph Auslander; "Definition" from *Poems of Inspiration and Courage* by Grace Noll Crowell, copyright 1936 by Harper & Brothers, renewed 1964 by Grace Noll Crowell.

Hill & Wang, Inc., for "To a Child with Eyes" from *Collected and New Poems: 1924-1963* by Mark Van Doren, copyright 1963 by Mark Van Doren.

Dr. Kenneth L. Hollenbeck, for "Hold Fast Your Dreams" by Louise Driscoll.

Houghton Mifflin Company, for "A Small Daughter Walking Outdoors" from *These Acres* by Frances M. Frost; "Wagon in the Barn" from *All About Me* by John Drinkwater; "A Song for My Mother — Her Stories" by Anna Hempstead Branch.

Alfred A. Knopf, Inc., for "Dreams" from *The Dream Keeper* by Langston Hughes, copyright 1932 by Alfred A. Knopf, Inc., renewed 1960 by Langston Hughes; "Be Not Afraid" (Autumn Sonnet #7) by Robert Nathan, copyright 1937, 1940, 1950 by Robert Nathan and "Bells in the Country" by Robert Nathan, copyright 1922, renewed 1950 by Robert Nathan (Both from *Green Leaf* by Robert Nathan); "Voices in the Staircase" from *New Poems 1960* by Witter Bynner, copyright 1960 by Witter Bynner; "Little Brother's Secret" by Katherine Mansfield, copyright 1924 by Alfred A. Knopf, Inc., renewed 1952 by John Middleton Murray (reprinted also by permission of The Society of Authors).

Paul Laune, for "The Gentleman Next Door" by Seigniora Laune.

Lawrence Levine, for "Dig We Must" from *Phoenix Nest, Saturday Review* edited by Martin Levin.

J. B. Lippincott Company, for "School-Bell" by Eleanor Farjeon, copyright 1938 by Eleanor Farjeon, renewed 1966 by Gervase Farjeon, and "Bedtime" by Eleanor Farjeon, copyright 1933, 1961 by Eleanor Farjeon (both from *Poems for Children* by Eleanor Farjeon); "I'm Wishing the Whole World Christmas" from *Days and Days* by Annette Wynne, copyright 1919, 1947 by Annette Wynne; "A Catch for Spring" from *Ardours and Endurances* by Robert Nichols; "To the Little House", "Animal Crackers" and "Songs for a Little House" from *Songs for a Little House* by Christopher Morley, copyright 1917, 1945 by Christopher Morley; "Smells" from *The Rocking Horse* by Christopher Morley, copyright 1919, 1947 by Christopher Morley.

Little, Brown & Company, for "The Morns Are Meeker Than They Were" from *The Complete Poems of Emily Dickinson*, edited by Thomas H. Johnson.

The Lyric, for "The Garden" by Carolyn Giltinan.

McGraw-Hill Book Company, for "The Little Whistler" by Frances Frost, copyright 1949 by McGraw-Hill, Inc.

The New York Times, for "A Prayer for Thanksgiving" by Joseph Auslander, copyright 1947 by The New York Times.

W. W. Norton & Company, Inc., for excerpt from *Where Did You Go? Out. What Did You Do? Nothing* by Robert Paul Smith, copyright 1957 by Robert Paul Smith.

Harold Ober Associates, Inc., for "Do You Save String?" from *Has Anyone Seen Me Lately?* by Corey Ford, copyright 1952 by Corey Ford.

G. P. Putnam's Sons, for "Little" from *Everything and Anything* by Dorothy Aldis, copyright 1925, 1926, 1927 by Dorothy Aldis.

Rand McNally & Company and Barbara Boyden Jordan, for "Mud" by Polly Chase Boyden from *Child Life Magazine* copyright 1930, 1958 by Rand McNally & Company.

Josephine Raney, for "Smells" from *Poems for Josephine* by Kathryn Worth, copyright 1943 by Kathryn Worth Curry.

Charles Scribner's Sons, for "Uncle Ananias" from *The Town Down the River* by Edwin Arlington Robinson, copyright 1910 by Charles Scribner's Son, renewed 1938 by Ruth Nivison; excerpt from "The White Bees" by Henry van Dyke, copyright 1909 by Charles Scribner's Sons, renewed 1937 by Tertius van Dyke.

Sheed and Ward, Inc., for "Daddy Fell into the Pond" from *Daddy Fell into the Pond and Other Poems* by Alfred Noyes, copyright 1952 by Alfred Noyes.

The Society of Authors, for "The Desire" by Katherine Tynan Hinkson; "Attic" by Rose Fyleman; "Dream-Song" from *Poems for Children* by Walter de la Mare; "Mother" from *Fairies and Chimneys* by Rose Fyleman.

The Viking Press, Inc., for "The Long Voyage" from *Blue Juniata: Collected Poems* by Malcolm Cowley, copyright 1938, renewed 1966 by Malcolm Cowley; "Piano" from *The Complete Poems of D. H. Lawrence,* Volume I, edited by Vivian de Sola Pinto and F. Warren Roberts, copyright 1920 by B. W. Huebsch, Inc., renewed 1948 by Frieda Lawrence (reprinted also by permission of Laurence Pollinger Ltd. and William Heinemann Ltd.); "Mumps" from *Under the Tree* by Elizabeth Madox Roberts, copyright 1922 by B. W. Huebsch, Inc., renewed 1950 by Ivor S. Roberts; for excerpt from "Reginald at the Carlton" from *The Short Stories of Saki* by H. H. Munro (reprinted also by permission of The Bodley Head).

Wesleyan University Press, for "Early Supper" from *Light and Dark* by Barbara Howes, copyright 1956 by Barbara Howes.

Dixie Willson, for "The Mist and All" from *Favorite Poems Old and New* edited by Helen Ferris.

Yale University Press, for "Parenthood" and "A Comparison" both from *Songs for Parents* by John Farrar, copyright 1921 by Yale University Press.